BIG
CITY
ATLAS

This edition first published in
the United Kingdom in 2020 by
Pavilion Children's Books,
an imprint of Pavilion Books
Group Limited
43 Great Ormond Street
London WC1N 3HZ

This hardback edition first
published in 2021

Originally published as *Big City
Explorer* by Pavilion Children's
Books in 2014

Layout © Pavilion Books, 2014
Illustrations and text ©
Maggie Li, 2014

The moral rights of the author
and illustrator have been
asserted.

ISBN: 978-1-84365-4605

10 9 8 7 6 5 4 3 2 1

Reproduction by
Rival Colour Ltd, UK

Printed and bound by
Toppan Leefung Ltd, China

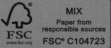

MIX
Paper from
responsible sources
FSC® C104723
FSC
www.fsc.org

BIG CITY ATLAS

JOIN PENGUIN ON A WORLD TOUR
OF 28 AMAZING CITIES!

BY MAGGIE LI

Toronto

14

10

Chicago

17

13

New York

San Francisco

6

8

Washington, D.C.

Mexico City

ATLANTIC OCEAN

KEY TO CONTINENTS

NORTH AMERICA
SOUTH AMERICA
AFRICA
EUROPE
ASIA
AUSTRALASIA
ANTARCTICA

20

Rio de Janeiro

19

Buenos Aires

PACIFIC OCEAN

N

NW   NE

W   E

SW   SE

S

CONTENTS

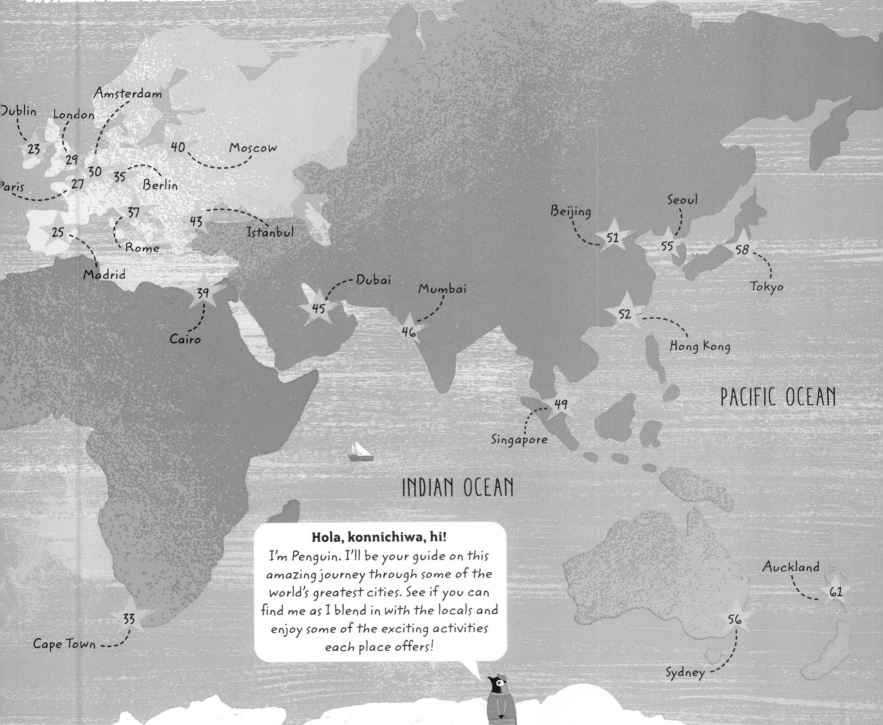

PACIFIC OCEAN

INDIAN OCEAN

Hola, konnichiwa, hi!
I'm Penguin. I'll be your guide on this amazing journey through some of the world's greatest cities. See if you can find me as I blend in with the locals and enjoy some of the exciting activities each place offers!

SAN FRANCISCO

GOLDEN GATE BRIDGE

Hi!

San Francisco is situated on the West Coast in the state of California. It was founded by the Spanish and grew big during the great California Gold Rush. Today, it is one of the most popular cities in the United States.

COUNTRY USA
CURRENCY U.S. Dollar
Language English
Population 883,300

PARK AT 90 DEGREES

The Golden Gate Bridge is the most recognizable sight in San Francisco. It is 3 miles (5 km) long and took nine years to build.

San Francisco is so hilly that cars sometimes have to park sideways to stop them from rolling down the hill!

GOLDEN GATE PARK

CABLE CAR

ALCATRAZ

Say hi to the sea lions at Fisherman's Wharf.

Alcatraz Island, or "The Rock" as locals call it, is an island off the coast of San Francisco that was once a prison for the most dangerous criminals in the United States.

NORTH BEACH

Pier 39

WANTED

The most famous inmate at Alcatraz was the gangster Al Capone.

FISHERMAN'S WHARF

LOMBARD STREET

The crookedest street in the world

CHINATOWN

The city's Chinatown has the largest community of Chinese people outside of China. It is where the fortune cookie was invented.

TRANSAMERICA PYRAMID

FORTUNE COOKIE FACTORY

MARKET STREET

MUSEUM OF MODERN ART

The San Francisco 49ers are one of the most famous football teams. The "49ers" was also the name given to the "prospectors," or gold hunters, who moved to the city during the gold rush of 1849.

HAIGHT-ASHBURY

Laidback San Francisco was famous for its hippie movement in the 1960s.

SAN FRANCISCO 49ERS

MEXICO CITY

Hola! (Oh-lah)

This vast, sprawling city in Central America was built by the Spanish on the site of the ancient Aztec city of Tenochtitlan. Today, the Spanish and Indian communities have blended together to create a colorful mix of traditions and cultures.

COUNTRY Mexico   **Language** Spanish
CURRENCY Mexican Peso   **Population** 8.9 million

The ancient Aztecs were a bloodthirsty crowd. They believed they had to sacrifice human lives to keep the sun gods happy and to help their crops to grow. They killed as many as 50,000 people a year (that's one every 10 minutes).

In Aztec times you could enjoy some of these tasty treats!

Aztec Shopping List
1 pound ants (extra crunchy)
5 large lizards
1 mixed bag of frogs and toads
2 ounces beetle grubs and caterpillars

Mexico is famous for its "fiestas," or lively parties. On November 2, The Day of the Dead, people remember friends and relatives who have died. Each family puts on a great banquet and lights candles to guide the spirits of the dead to the feast.

DAY OF THE DEAD FESTIVAL

CHAPULTEPEC PARK

ANGEL OF INDEPENDENCE

MEXICAN HAT DANCE

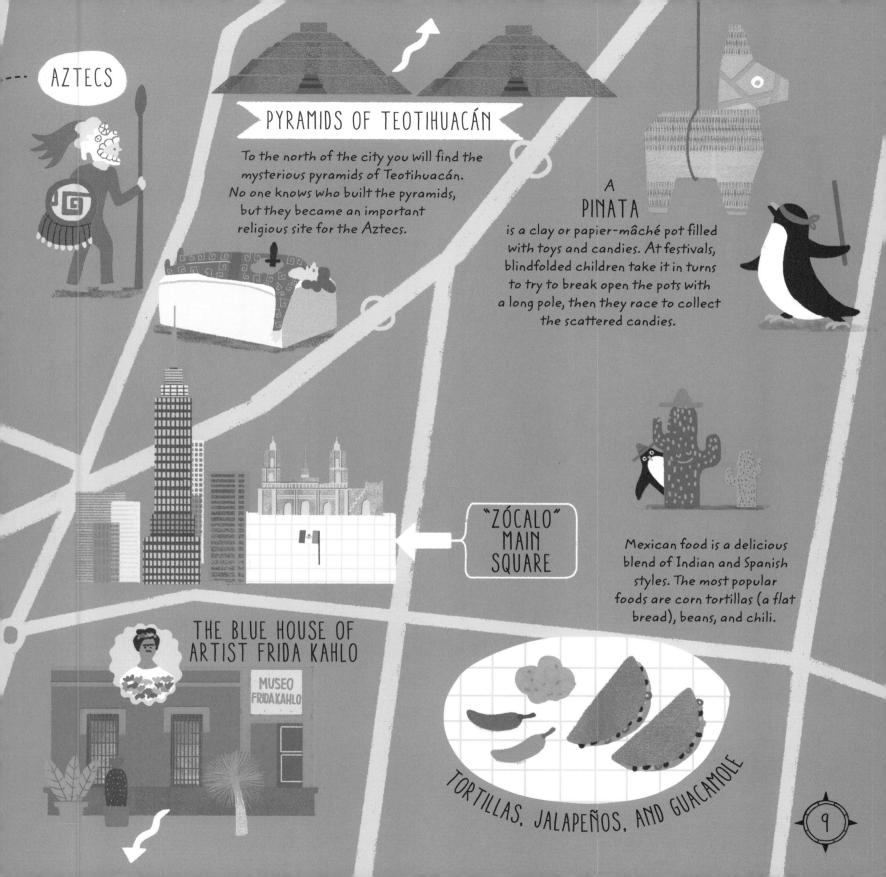

AZTECS

PYRAMIDS OF TEOTIHUACÁN

To the north of the city you will find the mysterious pyramids of Teotihuacán. No one knows who built the pyramids, but they became an important religious site for the Aztecs.

A **PINATA** is a clay or papier-mâché pot filled with toys and candies. At festivals, blindfolded children take it in turns to try to break open the pots with a long pole, then they race to collect the scattered candies.

"ZÓCALO" MAIN SQUARE

Mexican food is a delicious blend of Indian and Spanish styles. The most popular foods are corn tortillas (a flat bread), beans, and chili.

THE BLUE HOUSE OF ARTIST FRIDA KAHLO

MUSEO FRIDA KAHLO

TORTILLAS, JALAPEÑOS, AND GUACAMOLE

9

CHICAGO

Hey!
Chicago is in the U.S. state of Illinois. It is a beautiful city with skyscrapers rising above the waters of Lake Michigan, sandy beaches, and leafy parks. It is also the birthplace of the deep-dish pizza, the pinball machine, and the ferris wheel.

COUNTRY USA
CURRENCY U.S. Dollar
Language English
Population 2.7 million

At 1,450 feet (442 m), **WILLIS TOWER** is the United States' second tallest building.

Hold onto your hat! Chicago is known as the "windy city," because of the breezes that blow off Lake Michigan.

WINDY CITY

CHICAGO BULLS

Welcome to CHICAGO

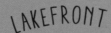

LAKEFRONT

Chicago's beautiful lakefront is a popular place to relax and play.

LAKE MICHIGAN

FIND IT
If you look carefully, you will find some of the amazing modern art sculptures that are dotted around the city.

The
GREEN MILL
Al Capone and other gangsters used to hang out at this famous jazz club in the 1920s.

DEEP-DISH PIZZA

The mouthwatering Chicago deep-dish pizza was created in 1943 by Ike Sewell, a former University of Texas football star.

NAVY PIER

DID YOU KNOW?
The first ferris wheel was constructed for the 1893 World's Fair in Chicago. Nothing of its kind had been seen before and it was huge. It stood 264 feet (80 m) high and held 1,400 passengers.

ABRAHAM
LINCOLN
1861–1865

THEODORE
ROOSEVELT
1901–1909

FRANKLIN D.
ROOSEVELT
1933–1945

JOHN F.
KENNEDY
1961–1963

BARACK
OBAMA
2009–2017

FAMOUS
RESIDENTS OF
THE WHITE HOUSE

THE WHITE HOUSE

Walk the halls and gardens once roamed by the former presidents and their first families. Look for President Lincoln's ghost, which is rumored to still live there!

WASHINGTON
MONUMENT

In 1912, the people of Japan sent more than 3,000 cherry trees to the city as a sign of their friendship with the United States.

LINCOLN MEMORIAL

DID YOU KNOW?
The city's motto is "Justitia Omnibus," which is Latin for "Justice for All."

POTOMAC RIVER

WASHINGTON, D.C.

EASTER EGG ROLL

Every year the President hosts an Easter egg rolling competition, where children race to push an egg along the lawn with a long spoon.

Hi!
The capital of the United States is known for its wide avenues, glistening monuments, and important government buildings. Its most famous site of all is the White House—home to U.S. presidents and a meeting place for world leaders since 1800.

COUNTRY USA
CURRENCY U.S. Dollar
Language English
Population 713,200

NATURAL HISTORY MUSEUM

SMITHSONIAN MUSEUMS

The U.S. Congress (government) meets here.

CAPITOL BUILDING

SUPREME COURT

NATIONAL AIR AND SPACE MUSEUM

The Smithsonian's 19 museums and galleries are crammed with all kinds of national treasures including a 3.5 billion-year-old fossil, the Apollo lunar landing module, and the original Star-Spangled Banner (American flag).

Washington takes its name from the United States' first president, George Washington. However, he is the only president not to have lived there.

THE UNITED STATES OF AMERICA
1
ONE DOLLAR

TORONTO

Hi!

Sprawled along the shore of beautiful Lake Ontario, Toronto is Canada's largest city. You can cycle the lakeside boardwalk, ride the ferry across to the islands, or paddle in a canoe. In winter, you can enjoy Canada's favorite pastimes: ice hockey and ice skating.

COUNTRY Canada
CURRENCY Canadian Dollar
Language English
Population 3 million

CANADIAN MOUNTED POLICE

MOUNTIES

MAPLE TREE

MAPLE SYRUP

The maple leaf is the national symbol of Canada and appears on the country's flag. Sap from the maple tree is used to make maple syrup, a popular topping on pancakes.

NATIONAL EXHIBITION

Every August millions of visitors head to the Canadian National Exhibition for carnival rides and lumberjack competitions.

Canada's largest museum contains many national treasures, including four totem poles carved from giant cedar trees by the First Nation people of Canada. Totem poles are a traditional way of telling stories and showing family "totems," which are objects thought to have special significance. They are placed in doorways to guard homes from evil.

FIRST NATIONS HEADDRESS

Native headdresses are community gifts that signify leadership

ROYAL ONTARIO MUSEUM

TORONTO MAPLE LEAFS ICE HOCKEY

CN TOWER

Climb to the top of the CN tower, one of the world's tallest freestanding towers, and enjoy the dizzying views of Toronto's skyline.

LAKE ONTARIO

A short ferry ride from downtown, this group of islands is completely car free and contains Centreville, an old-fashioned theme park with cotton candy and donkey rides.

TORONTO ISLANDS

Ellis Island was the gateway for millions of immigrants to the United States of America between 1892 and 1954. As they arrived, they would see the towering Statue of Liberty. The statue was a gift from France, built in 1886, and represents the independence and freedom of the country.

ELLIS ISLAND

ONE WORLD TRADE CENTER

BIG APPLE

STATUE OF LIBERTY

WALL ST

The famous financial district of New York

CHINATOWN

"Lady Liberty," as she is known, is so big that her nose is 4 feet 6 inches (132 cm) long and she wears a size 879 shoe.

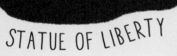
STATEN ISLAND

BROOKLYN BRIDGE

NYC

LITTLE ITALY

BROOKLYN

NEW YORK

EMPIRE STATE
BUILDING

Hi!
Did you know that New York City, also known as "The Big Apple," used to be the capital of the United States? It also has one of the world's most famous skylines, with towering skyscrapers that include the Empire State Building and the beautiful Chrysler Building.

COUNTRY USA   **Language** English
CURRENCY U.S. Dollar   **Population** 8.7 million

Broadway

HAPPY
NEW
YEAR!

CENTRAL PARK

TIMES SQUARE

CHRYSLER BUILDING

MANHATTAN

GUGGENHEIM
MUSEUM

NEW YORK
HOT DOG

New York City is made up of five districts: Manhattan, the Bronx, Brooklyn, Queens, and Staten Island. Manhattan sits in a natural harbor surrounded by water. New York City has many iconic attractions, from the bright lights of Times Square and Broadway, the home of musicals, to the world-famous Guggenheim Museum and New York Yankees baseball team.

THE BRONX

QUEENS

Many of Argentina's most important people are buried in this mini city for the dead, including Eva Péron, the wife of the former Argentine president.

LA RECOLETA

There are many "ferias," or outdoor markets, in Buenos Aires selling food, jewelry, and souvenirs.

BEEF

DID YOU KNOW?
In Argentina, they make dishes out of every part of the cow, even the stomach and the tongue.

This weekly fair is a celebration of Argentina's gaucho (cowboy) culture, with horse-riding competitions and delicious traditional foods, such as "empanadas" (meat-filled pies) and "choripán" (hot dogs).

Argentina's world-famous steaks come from cows that graze freely on grassy plains called "pampas."

PALACIO BAROLO

PALERMO

MONSERRAT

MATADEROS FAIR

PATO

The national sport of Argentina is a cross between basketball and polo. It is called "pato," which is the Spanish word for "duck," because in the early days the game was played with a live duck instead of a ball!

18

BUENOS AIRES

Top Things To Do
* Watch a Boca Juniors' soccer game
* Eat a juicy steak at a local "parrilla"
* Dance the tango!

Che! (Chay)
Buenos Aires is the beautiful and vibrant capital of Argentina. It has been called the "Paris of South America," because of its French-style buildings and cafés, and it is famous around the world for its mouthwatering steaks, soccer, and tango!

COUNTRY Argentina
CURRENCY Argentine Peso
Language Spanish
Population 2.9 million

CASA ROSADA

BOCA JUNIORS

SAN TELMO

CAMINITO

This famous dance began in the working class neighborhoods of Buenos Aires in the late nineteenth century. You can still see performers dancing in the streets today.

LA BOCA

TANGO

RIO DE JANEIRO

Brazilians are soccer crazy and their country has produced some of the best players. The most famous of all is Pelé.

Olá (Oh-lah)

Tropical "Rio" is Brazil's most famous city and its biggest tourist destination. With its majestic mountains topped with lush rain forest, sparkling blue sea, and white-sand beaches, it's no wonder it's known as the "cidade maravilhosa" (marvelous city).

COUNTRY Brazil
CURRENCY Brazilian Real
Language Portuguese
Population 6.7 million

TIJUCA FOREST

The world's biggest urban rain forest is filled with monkeys, birds, iguanas, waterfalls, caves, tropical plants, and giant trees.

FRESH FRUIT MARKETS

ATLANTIC OCEAN

The gorgeous beaches of Rio are famous throughout the world. Locals and tourists come here to swim, play soccer and volleyball, surf, and sunbathe.

IPANEMA BEACH

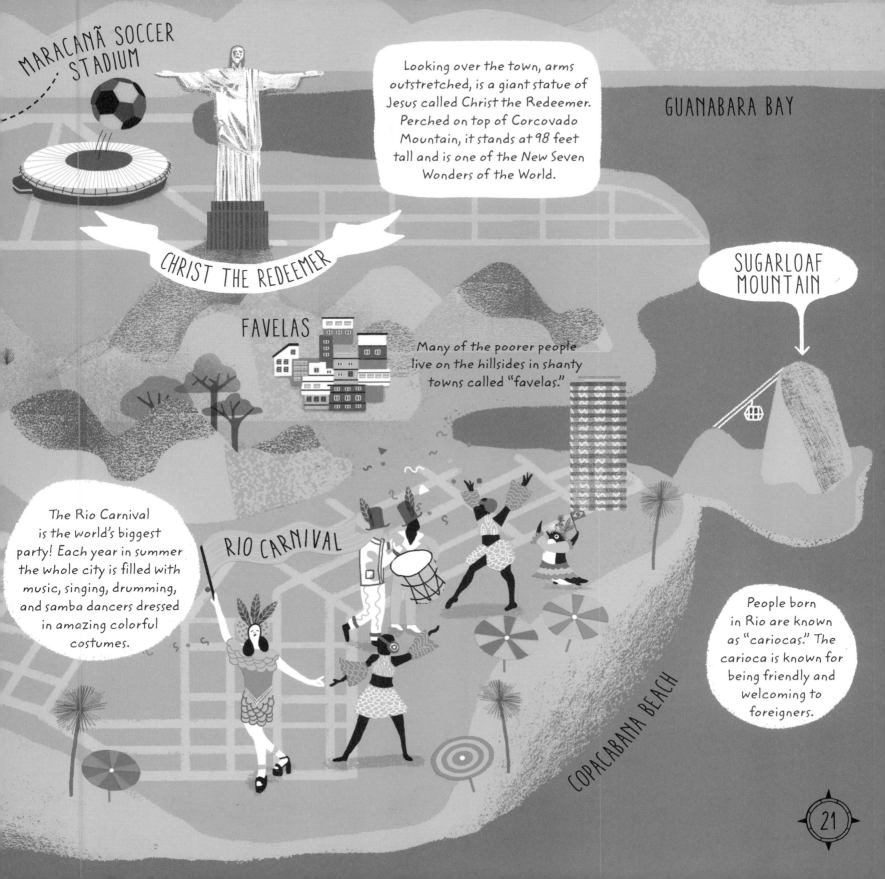

ACCORDION

TIN WHISTLE

BODHRAN

FIDDLE

IRISH DANCING

Irish music and dance has always been an important part of life for the people of Dublin.

The Irish have their own sports called hurling and Gaelic football.

VIKINGS

RIVER LIFFEY

Dublin was once the biggest Viking city outside of Scandinavia. Many people came to its busy port to trade silk, jewelry, spices, and other goods from all over Europe and as far away as Asia.

KILMAINHAM GAOL

FIND IT

Look for some of the Viking treasures that have been excavated from around the city.

Many people believe that this infamous jail is haunted by its former prisoners. Ghostly footsteps have been heard in the corridors, and in the chapel some people have seen the lights mysteriously turn themselves on and off.

DUBLIN

DUBLIN'S MOST FAMOUS WRITERS
James Joyce
Oscar Wilde
Bram Stoker

Hello!
The fair city of Dublin began life 1,000 years ago as a small Viking settlement on the banks of the River Liffey. Today, it is a friendly and lively city with a proud culture of Gaelic games, music, and dance.

COUNTRY Ireland
CURRENCY Euro
Language English, Irish
Population 1.3 million

DUBLINIA

This exciting museum will take you back in time to Viking and medieval Dublin. You can see what their houses looked like, what they wore, and what they ate. You can also listen to old Norse myths and sagas.

HA'PENNY BRIDGE

DUBLIN BAY

TRINITY COLLEGE

Dublin Castle has stood at the center of the city for 800 years. In medieval times the heads of invaders and rebels were mounted on spikes on the castle's walls to scare people away!

SAINT PATRICK'S DAY

March 17

Saint Patrick's Day is the feast day of the patron saint of Ireland. It is celebrated by Irish people throughout the world. The biggest parade is in New York City, and in Chicago they dye their river green!

GRAND CANAL

CHORIZO
AND JAMON

TAPAS

"Tapas" are small dishes that can include cheese, spicy Spanish sausage (chorizo), ham, seafood, and vegetables, such as tomatoes and olives.

MANZANARES RIVER

Madrid's city "plaza" has been a popular place for locals to meet for hundreds of years. The cobbled, medieval square was once the site of fiestas (parties), royal ceremonies, bullfights, and grisly executions.

GRAND VIA

ROYAL PALACE

PLAZA MAYOR

There are many palaces, cathedrals, and monasteries in the city. The magnificent Royal Palace is filled with rare treasures, including weapons, paintings, sculptures, and jewels.

EL RASTRO MARKET

SIESTA TIME

After lunch, it is traditional to take a short nap called a "siesta."

Madrid's busiest and oldest open-air market

MADRID

Hola! (Oh-lah)

Madrid is the capital of Spain and is home to the Spanish Royal family as well as the Spanish government. With its warm weather, great art treasures, dazzling cathedrals, and tasty tapas, it is one of Spain's best loved cities.

COUNTRY Spain
CURRENCY Euro
Language Spanish
Population 3.3 million

The Santiago Bernabéu Stadium is the home of one of the most successful clubs in world soccer, Real Madrid.

Flamenco is a type of traditional Spanish music and dance. It is known for its bright clothing and flamboyant moves. Ole!

In the middle of the city, in a busy square called Puerta del Sol, you will find a statue of a bear eating fruit from a tree. This is the symbol of Madrid and can be seen on its coat of arms.

PRADO MUSEUM

RETIRO PARK

The Moulin Rouge is the birthplace of can-can dancing, which can still be seen 120 years later. It was popular with artists who sketched and painted the dancers.

MOULIN ROUGE

 FIND IT

Paris is home to the Mona Lisa, the famous painting by Leonardo da Vinci. See if you can find it.

ARC DE TRIOMPHE

CHAMPS-ELYSEES

LOUVRE

The Palace of Versailles was the home of the kings and queens of France. It is the grandest palace in France, with a glittering hall of mirrors and magnificent gardens.

METRO

SEINE RIVER

EIFFEL TOWER

MONTPARNASSE

PARIS

SACRE COÉUR

TO LONDON

GARE DU NORD

MONTMARTRE

Bonjour! (Bon-zhoor)
Paris is a beautiful old city where you will find famous works of art and delicious food. Take a boat down the Seine River and see if you can find the statues of Notre Dame. Don't forget to climb up the Eiffel Tower, one of the most visited attractions in the world.

COUNTRY France
CURRENCY Euro
Language French
Population 2.2 million

French bakeries are called "boulangeries." Step inside and you will find long sticks of bread called baguettes and lovely buttery croissants.

NOTRE DAME

BASTILLE

ST-GERMAIN

CATACOMBS

These gruesome underground tunnels are filled with millions of bones and skulls. They were moved here about 200 years ago, because the graveyards had become overcrowded and smelly.

In 1789 the French peasants revolted against their rulers. The king and the nobles (rich people) were taken to the Bastille and their heads were cut off with a head-chopping machine called a "guillotine."

MIND THE GAP

Buckingham Palace is the official London home of the Queen. It has 775 rooms, 1,514 doors, and 760 windows!

SHERLOCK HOLMES

The London tube is the oldest underground system in the world. During World War II, Londoners slept in the tunnels to protect them from the bombing raids above them.

BUCKINGHAM PALACE

Big Ben is the name of the 13-ton bell inside the clock tower.

REMEMBER REMEMBER THE 5TH OF NOVEMBER!

In 1605 Guy Fawkes hatched a dastardly plan to blow up King James I and his parliament. The plot was uncovered just in time. The event is remembered each year on November 5 with fireworks and bonfires all across the country.

HOUSES OF PARLIAMENT

LONDON EYE

LONDON'S HIDDEN PAST

London was founded by the Romans in AD 46. The town was called Londinium and had fortified walls, baths, and an arena where savage gladiator fights took place. Evidence of London's Roman past can still be found, including skeletons and coins.

WHERE CAN I GO?

LONDON

The Tower of London is one of the most haunted places in the country. The ghost of Henry VIII's second wife, Anne Boleyn, who was beheaded in 1536, has been said to walk around the tower carrying her head under her arm!

Hello!
In its 2,000-year history, London has survived great fires, rebellions, and plagues. Join me on my red bus tour as I have a cup of tea with the Queen, watch the changing of the guards, and listen to tales of torture at the Tower of London.

COUNTRY England
CURRENCY British Pound
Language English
Population 8.7 million

ST PAUL'S CATHEDRAL

A traditional East End meal

PIE AND MASH

PEARLY KINGS AND QUEENS

TOWER OF LONDON

RIVER THAMES

TATE MODERN

DID YOU KNOW?
For 600 years, wild animals from around the world were kept in the tower, including a lion called Elizabeth and a grizzly bear called Martin!

THE SHARD

TOWER BRIDGE

CUTTY SARK

AMSTERDAM

Hallo! (Hal-low)

There is nowhere else like Amsterdam. With its winding canals and pretty bridges, it is full of character and charm. You can cycle the narrow streets or chug along in a canal boat, and in springtime the fields come alive with rainbow-colored tulips.

COUNTRY Netherlands
CURRENCY Euro
Language Dutch
Population 866,700

CAT BOAT
(poezenboot)

A floating home for stray cats.

NARROW HOUSE

Many of the city's houses are built on wooden poles to stop them from sinking into the canals.

HOUSE OF ANNE FRANK

Amsterdam is well known for its beautiful tulips, but, the first tulip bulbs actually came from Turkey!

During World War II, two Jewish families, the Franks and the von Peels, hid in this tiny secret apartment for two long years before being captured by the Nazis. The brave 13-year-old Anne Frank kept a diary of her time in hiding.

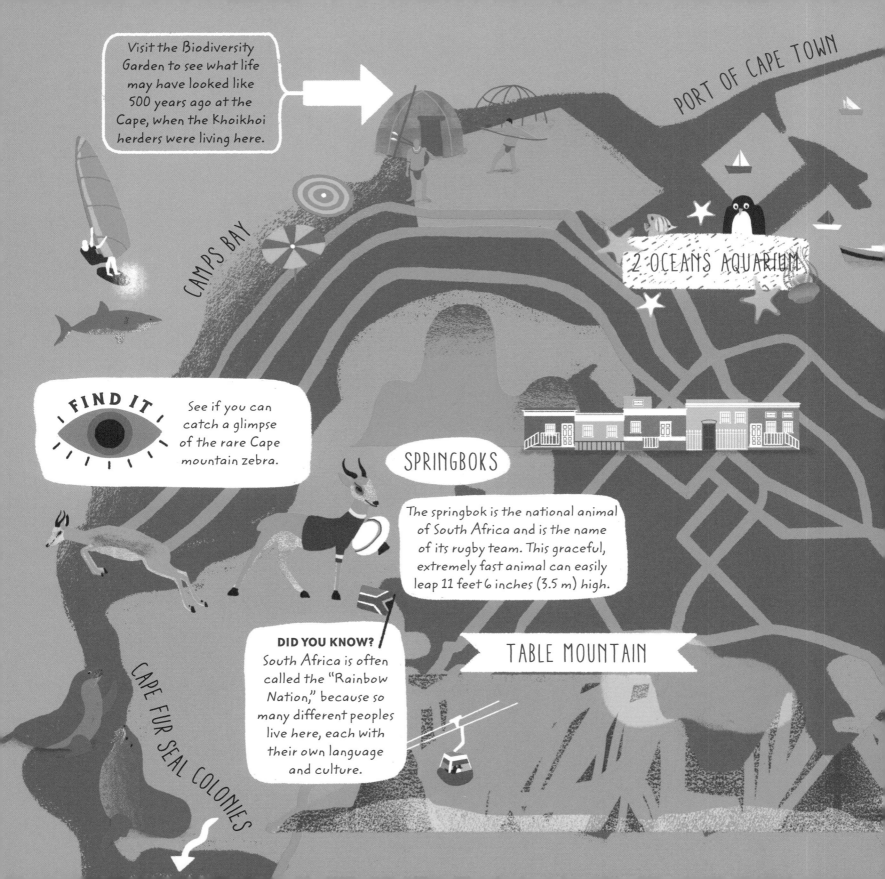

CAPE TOWN

At the popular V&A waterfront, you can watch lively performances by Cape jazz musicians, stilt walkers, and marching bands.

Hallo! (Hal-low)

With its beautiful national park, humpback whales, and mischievous baboons, Cape Town is a nature lover's paradise. Towering over the South African city is the magnificent flattop Table Mountain. Take a cable car to the top and admire the view!

COUNTRY South Africa
CURRENCY South African Rand

Language Afrikaans, English, Xhosa
Population 3.5 million

BRAAIS AND BILTONG

South Africans love their "braais" (barbecues). Another popular food is biltong, strips of dried meat that come in different flavors, such as beef, springbok, and ostrich.

CASTLE OF GOOD HOPE

Many animals roam around the Cape, including ostriches, bontebok (antelope), baboons, and the rare Cape mountain zebra. At the southern tip is Cape Point, which is where the mighty Indian and Atlantic oceans meet.

CAPE OF GOOD HOPE

DON'T FEED THE BABOONS!

GERMAN SAUSAGES

Germans love to eat sausages. They are usually served in a bread roll with mustard or sauerkraut (fermented cabbage). They come in all sizes—some are a whole yard (100 cm) in length!

Climb the dome of the famous Reichstag Parliament building for views across the city.

REICHSTAG

BRANDENBURG GATE

TIERGARTEN

CHRISTMAS MARKETS

Christmas is a magical time in Berlin. There are more than 60 traditional markets in the city selling handicrafts, hot chestnuts, and gingerbread cookies. The Potsdamer Platz market even has a toboggan run and an ice rink!

BERLIN

BERLIN TV TOWER

Guten Tag! (Goo-tehn-tahg)

Next stop, Berlin, Germany's capital city! Sitting prettily on the banks of the Spree River, this historic city is filled with amazing museums, palaces, and monuments. Don't forget to try one of their famous sausages—there are more than 1,000 varieties to choose from.

COUNTRY Germany
CURRENCY Euro
Language German
Population 3.5 million

MUSEUM ISLAND

Lederhosen are leather shorts traditionally worn by German men and boys.

HOLOCAUST MEMORIAL

This important monument was built in memory of the millions of Jews who were killed by Hitler and his forces during World War II.

SPREE RIVER

During the Cold War (1961–1989), the city was divided in two by the Berlin Wall. Many people were shot trying to escape from the eastern part to the western part. The fall of the wall in 1989 was a famous moment in history. Friends and families were reunited for the first time in years and there were great celebrations throughout Germany.

BUDDY BEAR

Buddy Bear is the city's symbol and mascot. Statues of Buddy can be found all around the city.

BERLIN WALL

FREEDOM

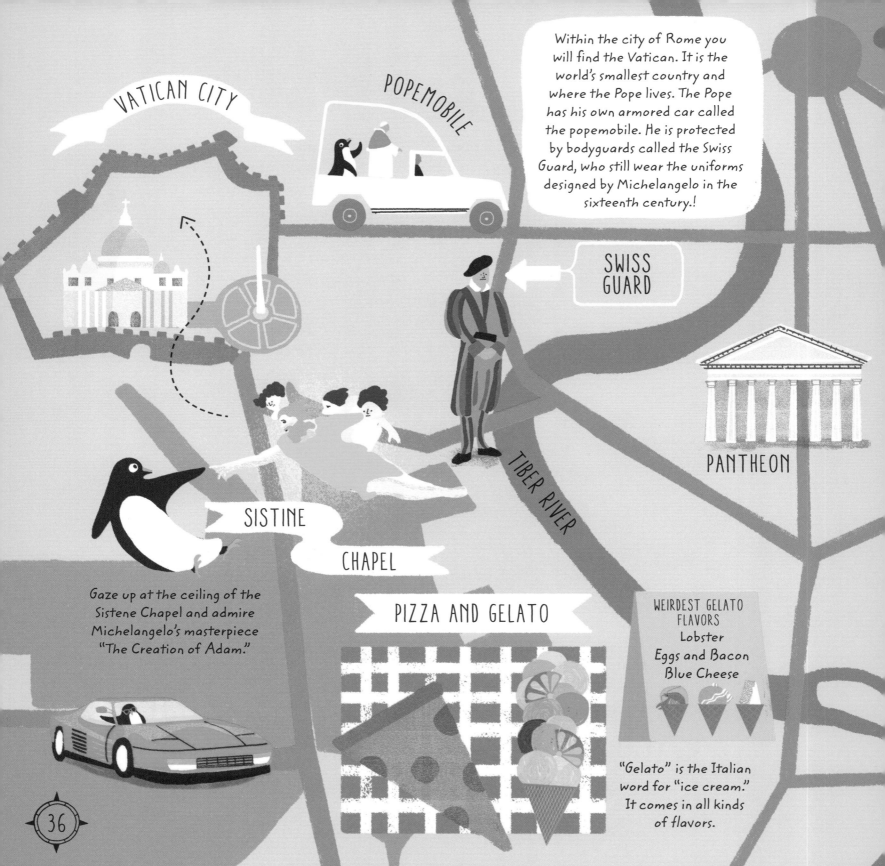

VATICAN CITY

POPEMOBILE

Within the city of Rome you will find the Vatican. It is the world's smallest country and where the Pope lives. The Pope has his own armored car called the popemobile. He is protected by bodyguards called the Swiss Guard, who still wear the uniforms designed by Michelangelo in the sixteenth century.!

SWISS GUARD

PANTHEON

TIBER RIVER

SISTINE CHAPEL

Gaze up at the ceiling of the Sistene Chapel and admire Michelangelo's masterpiece "The Creation of Adam."

PIZZA AND GELATO

WEIRDEST GELATO FLAVORS
Lobster
Eggs and Bacon
Blue Cheese

"Gelato" is the Italian word for "ice cream." It comes in all kinds of flavors.

ROME

The ancient Romans looked like this.

Buongiorno! (Bwon-jor-no)
Once the center of the mighty Roman Empire, Rome contains a treasure trove of ancient monuments and great works of art, from the mighty Colosseum to Michelangelo's paintings in the Sistine Chapel. It is also home to the head of the Catholic Church, the Pope!

COUNTRY Italy
CURRENCY Euro
Language Italian
Population 2.6 mllion

TREVI FOUNTAIN

The Trevi Fountain was built in 1762. Every day crowds come here to throw coins into the fountain's water for good luck.

Many kinds of exotic beasts were brought to the Colosseum to fight, including crocodiles, giraffes, tigers, and lions. Sometimes they flooded the arena and put on mock sea battles using real ships.

Crowds filled the Colosseum to watch plays and gladiator fights. Gladiators were usually slaves or criminals who were trained to fight each other, or wild animals, to the death.

COLOSSEUM

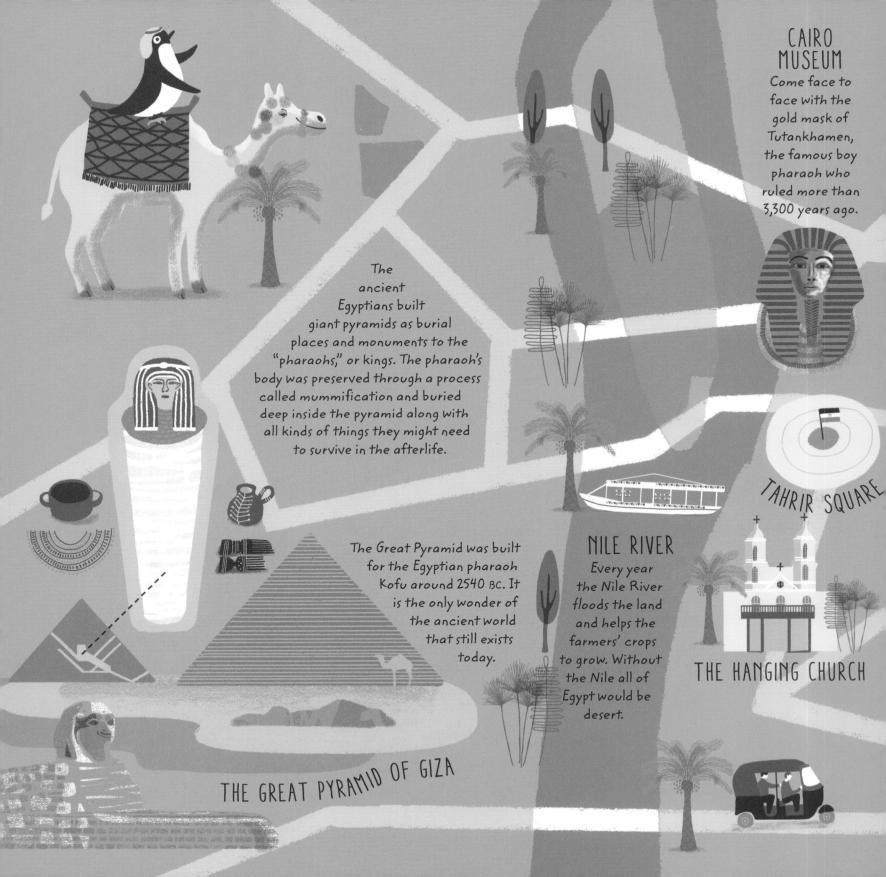

CAIRO MUSEUM
Come face to face with the gold mask of Tutankhamen, the famous boy pharaoh who ruled more than 3,300 years ago.

The ancient Egyptians built giant pyramids as burial places and monuments to the "pharaohs," or kings. The pharaoh's body was preserved through a process called mummification and buried deep inside the pyramid along with all kinds of things they might need to survive in the afterlife.

The Great Pyramid was built for the Egyptian pharaoh Kofu around 2540 BC. It is the only wonder of the ancient world that still exists today.

NILE RIVER
Every year the Nile River floods the land and helps the farmers' crops to grow. Without the Nile all of Egypt would be desert.

TAHRIR SQUARE

THE HANGING CHURCH

THE GREAT PYRAMID OF GIZA

CAIRO

Ahlan! (Ah-lan)
Exploring Egypt's ancient city of Cairo is like stepping back in time. Its narrow, dusty streets are a maze of mosques and stores selling everything from live chickens to tourist trinkets. Hitch a ride on a camel and go in search of the magnificent pyramids and treasures of the pharaohs!

COUNTRY Egpyt
CURRENCY Egyptian Pound
Language Egyptian Arabic
Population 9.1 million

The domes and minarets of the city's mosques rise up into the sky. A minaret is a tall tower from which a "muezzin," or crier, summons the people to prayer. The sound of this call floats across the rooftops and can be heard throughout the city.

Watch the spectacular twirling dance of the whirling dervishes at the medieval citadel.

Many of the city's poorer families have moved into the city's cemeteries, where they have turned the tombs and mausoleums into homes.

CITADEL

CITY OF THE DEAD

MOSCOW

Privyet! (Pree-vyet)

Moscow is a city with a colorful past, from marauding Mongols and revolution, to the birth of space travel. With its fairytale palaces and beautiful Bolshoi Ballet, there's plenty to see and do.

COUNTRY Russia
CURRENCY Rouble
Language Russian
Population 11 million

ST. BASIL'S CATHEDRAL

was built in 1561 by the scary Russian leader Ivan the Terrible. It has rainbow-colored domes built to look like flames rising into the sky.

RED SQUARE

KREMLIN

This is where the President of Russia lives.

PUSHKIN MUSEUM

MOSKVA RIVER

Russians love chess. It is a national sport with tournaments across the country.

CHESS

DONSKOY MONASTERY

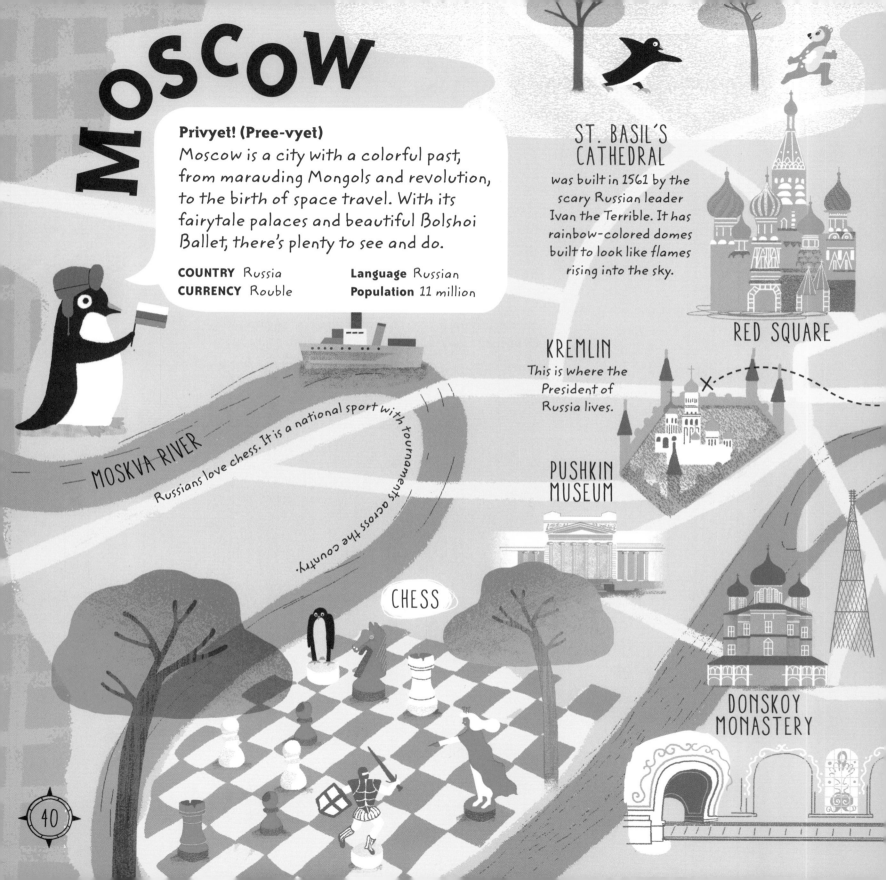

The
BOLSHOI BALLET
is one of the oldest
and most famous ballet
schools in
the world.

LAIKA

In 1957 a dog called
Laika became the first
living creature to orbit
Earth, leading the way
for human space travel.
She was a stray dog,
found on the streets of
Moscow.

The
MEMORIAL MUSEUM OF COSMONAUTICS
contains the capsule used
by the Russian cosmonaut Yuri
Gagarin, who was the first person
to go into space.

LENIN'S MAUSOLEUM

Watch the flying trapeze artists,
clowns, and acrobats at the world-
renowned Moscow State Circus.

The
MOSCOW METRO
is the world's most
decorative subway.
Its platforms and
stations were built as
"palaces for the people"
filled with mosaics,
statues, and stained glass.

BLINIS AND CAVIAR
Russians like to eat
blinis (mini pancakes)
with caviar, which
are the eggs of
sturgeon, a type
of fish.

CIRCUS

HAMAM

"Hamam," or public baths, have been an important part of Turkish life for hundreds of years.

"Bazaar" is the Turkish name for an open-air market. It contains many stores selling traditional items, such as carpets, silk slippers, exotic spices, and a famous candy flavored with rose petals called Turkish delight.

GOLDEN HORN

GRAND BAZAAR

A "simit" is a round Turkish bread similar to a pretzel. Street sellers carry huge trays of them on their heads like this.

Istanbul has had many different names over the years including Byzantium, Constantinople, and Stamboul.

MEZE PLATTER

Popular Turkish foods include kebabs made from broiled lamb, hummus (a dip make from chickpeas), and baba ganoush (mashed eggplants).

ISTANBUL

GALATA

Merhaba! (Mehr-hah-bah)
Turkey's Istanbul is one the greatest and most ancient cities. Once a bustling trading port, the city has been the capital of the powerful Roman, Byzantine, and Ottoman empires. Visitors today come to haggle in its open-air markets and admire its magnificent buildings.

COUNTRY Turkey
CURRENCY Turkish Lira
Language Turkish
Population 13.3 million

TOPKAPI PALACE
This is where the "sultans," or kings once lived.

HAGIA SOPHIA

BOSPHORUS

EUROPE

ASIA

Istanbul is the only city in the world that straddles two continents. Its western side is in Europe but hop on a ferry or cross the bridge over the Bosphorus River and you will find yourself in Asia.

BLUE MOSQUE

THE WORLD
ISLANDS

THE PALM ISLANDS

The Palm Islands and the World
Islands are a group of amazing
man-made islands in the
PERSIAN GULF

JUMEIRAH
MOSQUE

BURJ AL
ARAB

FIND IT See if you can find
Dubai's record-
breaking buildings.

World's tallest man-made structure
Burj Khalifa
World's biggest shopping mall
The Dubai Mall
World's most luxurious hotel
The seven-star Burj Al Arab

BURJ KHALIFA

At these curious contests,
camels are judged on foot size,
eyelash length, nobility, and
build. The longer the eyelashes,
the better the protection
against sandstorms.

THE DUBAI MALL

Falcons have been used for hunting in
Dubai for centuries and are treated
with great care. People often buy an
extra business class seat on the plane
when they are traveling so that their
falcons can sit alongside them.

2   1   3
CAMEL BEAUTY CONTEST

DUBAI

The most common greeting in Dubai is:
As-salaa-mu alai kum
(May peace be upon you)
The reply is always:
Wa alai kum as-salaam
(and peace be upon you, too)

Dubai is like nowhere else on the planet. It is one of the world's fastest-growing and most futuristic cities, with spectacular skyscrapers and glamorous island resorts. It is also a city with a rich Arab heritage and culture with glistening mosques, bustling souks, and camel beauty contests!

COUNTRY United Arab Emirates
CURRENCY Dirham
Language Arabic
Population 2.8 million

Many men wear the "kandura," a full-length white shirtdress. Women wear a long black robe called an "abaya" and cover their hair with a "hijab," or scarf.

There are "souks," or stores, of every kind in Dubai. There is a perfume souk, a food souk, a spice souk, a textile souk, and even a glittering gold souk.

SOUKS

The traditional sport of camel racing is popular in Dubai. Instead of people, they use tiny remote-controlled robot jockeys!

CAMEL RACECOURSE

MUMBAI

Namaste! (Na-ma-ste)

Next stop Mumbai, the gateway to India. Once a small fishing village, this colorful and chaotic city is now one of the biggest urban sprawls on the planet. Jump into a tuk-tuk or squeeze onto one of the local trains and take in all the exotic sights and smells!

COUNTRY India
CURRENCY Indian Rupee
Language Hindi
Population 20.2 million

When Indian people greet each other, they place their hands together and say "Namaste." This means "I bow my head to you."

A CITY OF TWO HALVES

Mumbai is India's wealthiest city, but it is also home to some of the world's poorest people. This maze of shacks and narrow alleyways is one of the city's largest shanty towns.

DHARAVI

Mumbai is famous for its delicious spicy street food. A popular traditional snack is "pav bhaji," a vegetable curry in an Indian roll.

SIDDHIVINAYAK TEMPLE

FIND IT

Can you spy the elephant-headed Lord Ganesha? This popular Hindu god has large ears to listen, a big head to think, and a fat belly to eat all the bad things in the world.

VICTORIA TERMINUS

GATEWAY TO INDIA

BOLLYWOOD

Mumbai is the birthplace of "Bollywood," India's all-singing, all-dancing movie industry.

CHOWPATTY BEACH

Keep your eyes peeled for the "dabbawalas" in their white caps and baggy pants as they carry home-cooked lunches to schools and offices all across the city.

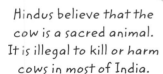

Hindus believe that the cow is a sacred animal. It is illegal to kill or harm cows in most of India.

"Diwali," or the Festival of Lights, marks the beginning of the Indian New Year and is Mumbai's biggest Hindu celebration.

DIWALI

47

This strange prickly fruit called durian is so smelly it is banned from public transportation and some hotels!

Things you CAN'T do in Singapore
1. No littering
2. No selling gum
3. No durian

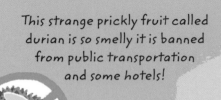

In this amazing zoo, animals roam freely in enclosures that copy their natural habitats. Many endangered species live here, such as the Malayan tiger and orangutans.

SINGAPORE ZOO

MALAYSIA

JURONG BIRD PARK

HAWKER CENTER

The four main ethnic groups in Singapore are the Malays, Chinese, Indians, and Eurasians.

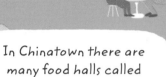

In Chinatown there are many food halls called hawker centers, where you can try popular local dishes, such as chicken rice.

SINGAPORE

Hello!

Singapore isn't just a city—it is actually a small country. It is home to many different ethnic groups, each with their own cultures and religions. You can visit Hindu temples and ancient Buddhist shrines, or join in the many different festivals that are celebrated through the year.

COUNTRY Singapore
CURRENCY Singapore Dollar

Language English, Malay, Chinese, and Tamil
Population 5.8 million

SERANGOON ROAD

LITTLE INDIA

SULTAN MOSQUE

In Little India you will find Hindu temples, Indian restaurants, and street stalls selling flower garlands and "saris," or Indian dresses.

MARINA BAY SANDS

The Colonial District dazzles with beautiful nineteenth-century buildings, including the famous Raffles Hotel.

On the roof of this luxurious hotel, 650 feet (200 m) in the air, is a swimming pool shaped like a boat.

FIND IT

Can you spot the rare and colourful Oriental Pied Hornbill bird?

The Great Wall of China is the longest man-made object in the world and can be seen from space! It was built more than 2,000 years ago to stop enemies from invading the city.

GREAT WALL

According to legend, there was once a wild beast called Nian that appeared at the end of each year, attacking and killing villagers. Loud noises and fires were used to scare the creature away, and so began the Chinese New Year festival. Today, it is the most important holiday in China and is celebrated with decorations, feasting, fireworks, and the lighting of lanterns.

CHINESE NEW YEAR

BEIJING ZOO

The ancient Chinese invented many things we still use today, including gunpowder, the compass, the abacus, paper, ink, porcelain china, the wheelbarrow, and the folding umbrella.

MOSCOW

BEIJING

TRANS-SIBERIAN RAILWAY

The longest train journey in the world

INVENTIONS

Nihao! (Nee-how)

This ancient Chinese city is famed for its Great Wall, temples, and palaces. Right at its center is the mysterious Forbidden City. Built by a million workers, this imperial palace contains more than 980 buildings and was home to Chinese emperors for 500 years.

COUNTRY China
CURRENCY Yuan

Language Chinese (Mandarin)
Population 21 million

BIRD'S NEST STADIUM

FORBIDDEN CITY

This magnificent fifteenth-century Ming Dynasty tower was once used to perform animal sacrifices to the gods. Today, you will find hundreds of locals in the surrounding park practicing t'ai chi (a Chinese martial art), playing the "erhu" (a kind of violin), and singing Chinese opera.

BEIJING OPERA

TEMPLE OF HEAVEN

ERHU

The Chinese have been using chopsticks since at least AD 400. They use them to grip their food like a pair of tweezers.

HONG KONG

MAINLAND CHINA

Haa lo! (Haa-lo)

High-tech buildings and neon signs sit side by side with traditional ramshackle houses, ancient temples, and shrines in the bustling city of Hong Kong. This former British colony lies on the south coast of continental China and has the largest number of skyscrapers in the world, almost twice as many as New York.

COUNTRY China
CURRENCY Hong Kong Dollar

Language Chinese (Cantonese), English
Population 7.4 million

NEW TERRITORIES

I SPY

Can you see the Big Buddha statue? It stands 112 feet (34 m) tall and can be seen from far away.

STAR FERRY

JUNKS

Victoria Harbor was once visited by pirates and smugglers. Today, you will find thousands of tourists and city workers crossing between Kowloon and Victoria on the Star Ferry.

Traditional Chinese festivals are an important part of modern Hong Kong life. During the annual Cheung Chau Bun festival, hundreds of men race to the top of a giant tower of steamed buns. It is believed that the more buns they snatch, the better fortune they will bring their family.

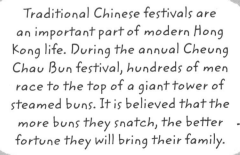

LANTAU ISLAND

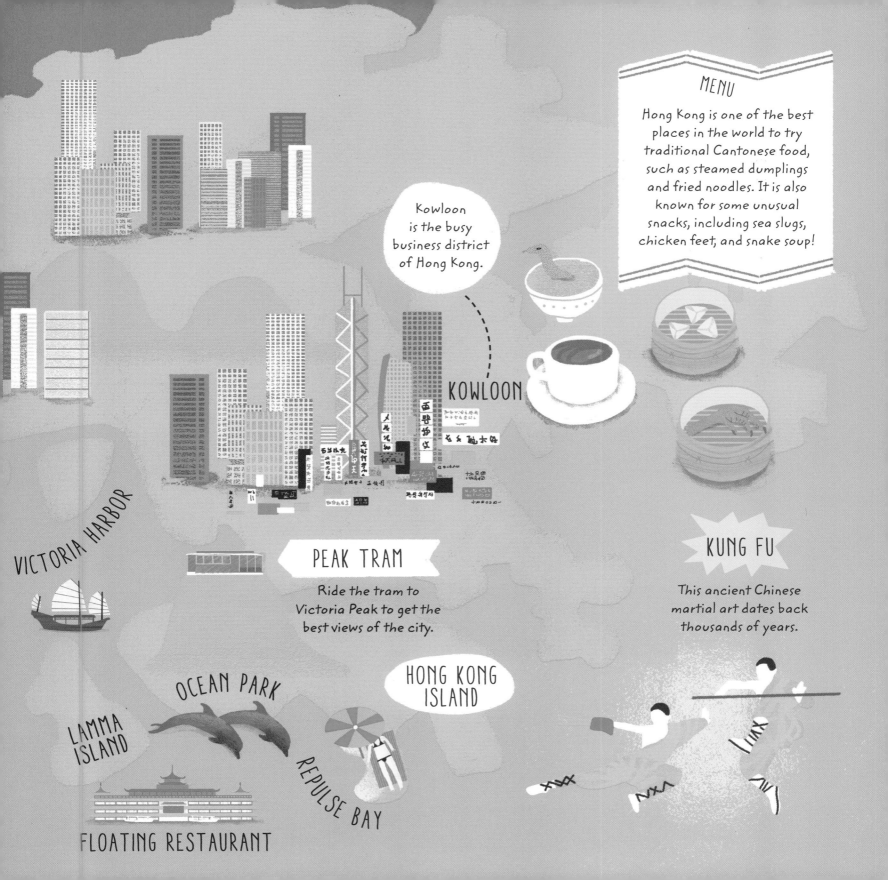

Kowloon is the busy business district of Hong Kong.

MENU

Hong Kong is one of the best places in the world to try traditional Cantonese food, such as steamed dumplings and fried noodles. It is also known for some unusual snacks, including sea slugs, chicken feet, and snake soup!

KOWLOON

VICTORIA HARBOR

PEAK TRAM

Ride the tram to Victoria Peak to get the best views of the city.

KUNG FU

This ancient Chinese martial art dates back thousands of years.

OCEAN PARK

LAMMA ISLAND

HONG KONG ISLAND

REPULSE BAY

FLOATING RESTAURANT

THE FOUR MOUNTAINS

Residents of Seoul believe that they are protected by the four sacred mountains that surround the city. In ancient times a huge fortress wall connected them together and kept invaders out. Parts of the wall are still standing and can be seen today.

MT. BUGAKSAN

GYEONGBOKGUNG PALACE

GWANGHWAMUN GATE

MT. INWANGSAN

MASCOT HAECHI

Yongsan is a huge shopping mall filled with more than 5,000 stores. Here, you can pick up all the electronics you need from computers to washing machines.

YONGSAN ELECTRONICS

오시
해기
우세
G세이

FIND IT

Seoul's mascot is "haechi," a creature from Korean mythology with a lion's body and a unicorn's horn. There are statues of haechi all around the city. See how many you can find.

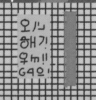

54

SEOUL

Annyeong haseyo! (An-nyoung-ha-sae-yo)
Busy modern life and quiet ancient traditions blend together in Seoul, a city full of unique culture. Climb up Mt. Namsan to see the views from the tower or visit a traditional Hanok village to try kite making, calligraphy, and kimchi pickling.

COUNTRY South Korea   **Language** Korean
CURRENCY Won   **Population** 11.5 million

BUKCHON HANOK VILLAGE

MT. NAKSAN

NAMSAN TOWER

MT. NAMSAN

FOOD AND CULTURE
Seoul has a rich culture of arts and crafts as well as being known for its delicious cuisine. Koreans have a lot of dishes during meal times. The most famous is a side dish called "kimchi," spicy fermented cabbage. There are hundreds of varieties to choose from.

According to Buddhist beliefs, lanterns symbolize wisdom. Each year, during the Lotus Lantern Festival, the city celebrates Buddha's birthday by lighting thousands of lanterns shaped like lotus flowers.

HAN RIVER

SYDNEY

G'day mate! (Gu-dei)

Surf boards at the ready and it's time to hit the beaches of sunny Sydney. There is a lot to love about this laidback city. People from all over the world come to admire its spectacular opera house and glistening harbor, koalas, and kangaroos.

COUNTRY Australia
CURRENCY Australian Dollar

Language English
Population 5 million

DID YOU KNOW?
Thanks to their strong legs and big feet, kangaroos can leap three to four times their own length in one hop, but they can't walk backward!

SYDNEY HARBOUR BRIDGE

THE ROCKS

SYDNEY OPERA HOUSE

DARLING HARBOUR

The Aboriginal people have inhabited the area now known as Sydney for more than 20,000 years. They have their own flag, which represents their relationship with the land.

Get up close to some of Australia's amazing animals. Hop along with the kangaroos, cuddle a koala, and wrestle a crocodile!

TARONGA ZOO

Between May and November pods of humpback whales breach the water in the harbor as they migrate along the coast.

BOTANICAL GARDENS

The first European settlers arrived in Sydney in January 1788 aboard the ships of the "First Fleet." The ships carried convicts who were sent here because Britain's prisons were so overcrowded.

AWESOME!

BONDI BEACH

SURF'S UP!

TOKYO

Konnichiwa! (Kon-ee-chee-wa)
Tokyo began as a small fishing village called Edo around 5,000 years ago. Today, it is the capital of Japan and one of the biggest, most populated cities in the world.

COUNTRY Japan **LANGUAGE** Japanese
CURRENCY Yen **POPULATION** 14 million

MYTHS AND LEGENDS
According to ancient legends, the city's rivers are home to a strange beast called a "kappa." A kappa is a turtlelike creature that enjoys kidnapping children and drowning swimmers. But don't worry. They can be won over by offerings of their favorite food—cucumbers!

Traditional Japanese outfits are called "kimonos." The name means "thing to wear."

SHIBUYA
The city's busy shopping district

IMPERIAL PALACE
Where the Emperor lives

TOKYO TOWER

MT. FUJI
Mount Fuji is an active volcano and the highest mountain in Japan. On a clear day it can be seen from the Sky Tree.

FISH MARKET
"Sushi" is the national dish of Japan. It is made from raw fish wrapped in rice and seaweed.

AUCKLAND

RANGITOTO ISLAND

Kia Ora! (Key-or-ra)
Welcome to Auckland, New Zealand's largest city. Join me as I sail around volcanic islands, climb rolling green hills, and come face to face with Maori warriors as they perform their fearsome "haka" war dance.

COUNTRY New Zealand **Language** English
CURRENCY NZ Dollar **Population** 1.4 million

MAORI CULTURE

AUCKLAND MUSEUM

AUCKLAND HARBOUR

See the amazing collection of Maori "taonga," or treasures, at the Auckland Museum.

THE DOMAIN

VOLCANIC CITY
The city is dotted with 48 volcanic cones. They are now covered with grass and look like large hills.

Maori people are thought to have first settled in Auckland about 1,000 years ago. They came from the Pacific Islands and traveled the seas in big canoes called "wakas." Today, you can experience traditional Maori culture by visiting a "marae," or meeting place, and having a celebratory feast cooked in a "hangi," or earthern oven.

The kiwifruit got its name from its similarity to the New Zealand kiwi bird. Both are brown and fuzzy on the outside.

ONE TREE HILL

SUPERCITY MATCHUP

Can you match the penguins to the correct landmarks?

2,700 ft.

1

2

3

4

5

a

b

c

d

e

2,600 ft.

2,000 ft.

1,300 ft.

65 ft.

30 ft.

6   7   8   9   10

f   g   h   i   j

63

SUPERCITY ROUNDUP

WHERE AM I?

1. Hallo! (Hal-low)

2. Ahlan! (Ah-lan)

3. Kia Ora! (Key-or-ra)

ANSWERS: 1. Amsterdam, 2. Cairo, 3. Auckland

FOOD GLORIOUS FOOD!

Can you remember where you might try these delicious treats?

1. Pie and Mash
2. Sausages and sauerkraut
3. Tapas
4. Biltong
5. Lobster-flavored gelato!

ANSWERS: 1. London, 2. Berlin, 3. Madrid, 4. Cape Town, 5. Rome

FESTIVALS AROUND THE WORLD

Where might you celebrate these festivals?

1. Day of the Dead
2. Diwali
3. Lotus Lantern Festival
4. St. Patrick's Day
5. Cheung Chau Bun Festival

ANSWERS: 1. Mexico City 2. Paris, 3. Mumbai 3. Seoul 4. Dublin 5. Hong Kong

PENGUIN FINDER

Did you find penguin in all his disguises?
Can you name which cities these are from?

1

2

3

4

5

ANSWERS: 1. San Francisco, 2. Paris, 3. Seoul, 4. Tokyo, 5. Washington, D.C.

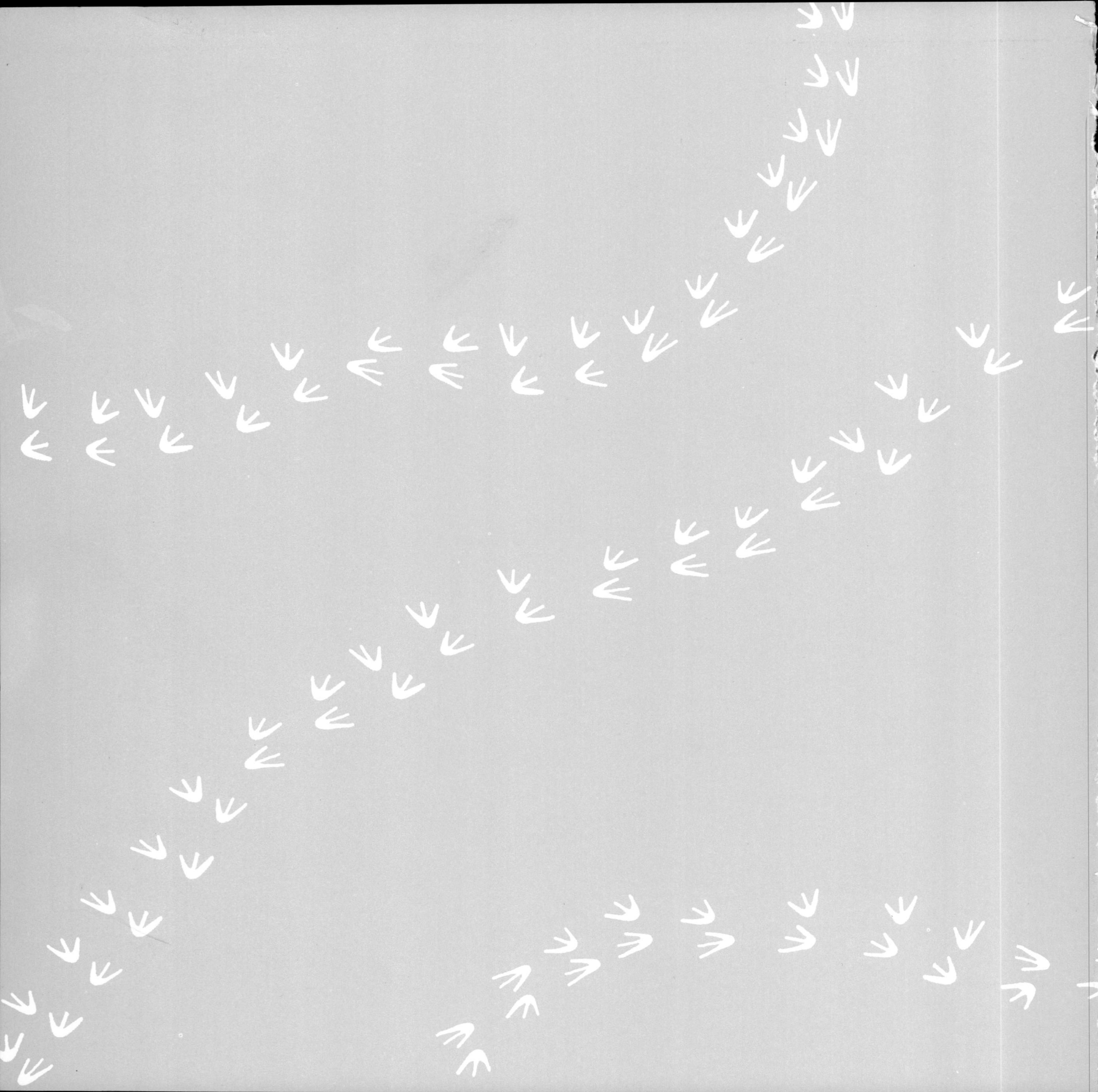